Trace each line from the fish to its twin.

Trace and print each capital letter.

A B

C D

E F

G H

I J

Trace and print each capital letter.

K L

M N

O P

Q R

S T

Trace and print each capital letter.

U V

W X

Y Z

Connect the dots. Begin at the ★ with the letter A. Continue in alphabetical order.

Trace and print each lowercase letter.

a b

c d

e f

g h

i j

Connect the dots. Begin at the ★ with the letter a. Continue in alphabetical order.

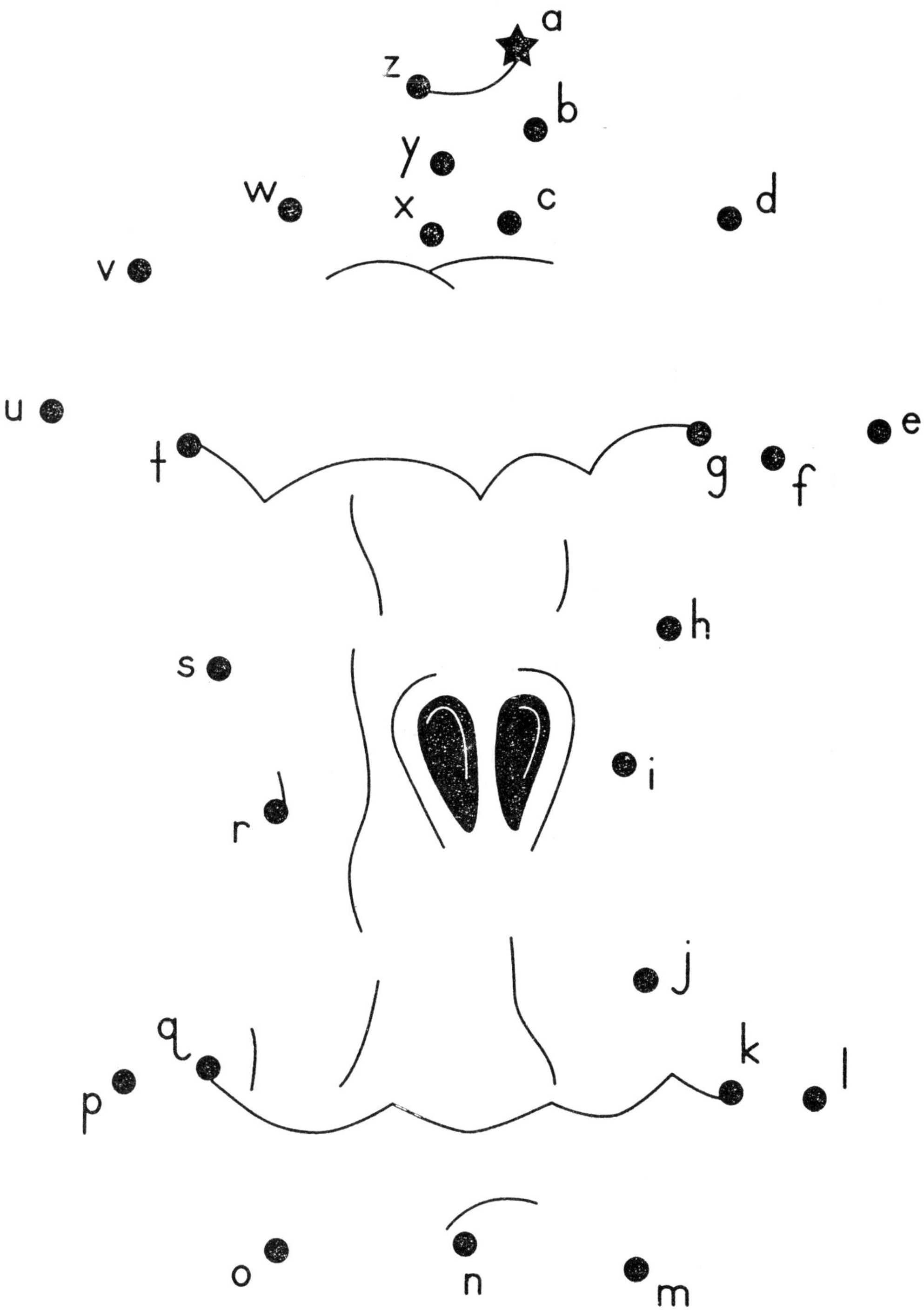

Print the correct lowercase letter next to each capital leter.
Trace the first letter that has been done for you.

A a

B

C

D

E

F

G

H

I

J

Print the correct capital letter next to each lowercase letter. Trace the first letter that has been done for you.

K k

l

m

n

o

p

q

r

s

t

Print the correct capital or lowercase letter next to each letter.

U

v

W

X

y

z

Complete each sentence.

My first name is

My last name is

I like

Trace each colour word and colour the picture next to it.

red

orange

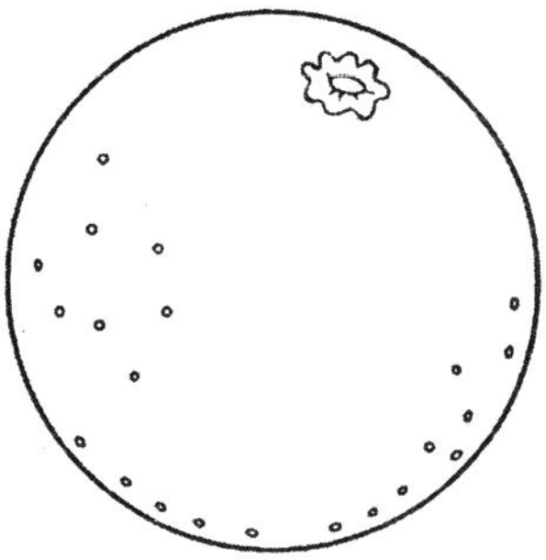

yellow

green

Trace each colour word and colour the picture next to it.

blue

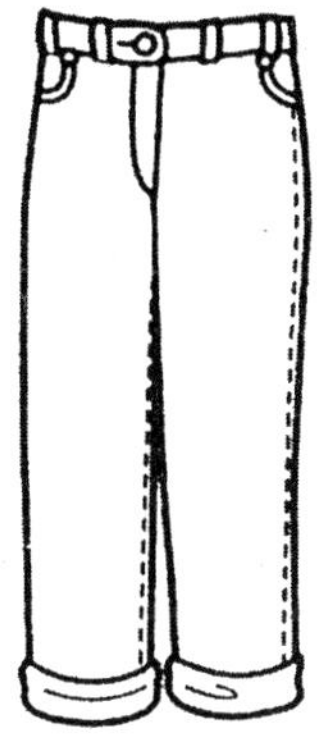

purple

brown

black

Draw a line from each picture to the letter that has the same beginning sound.

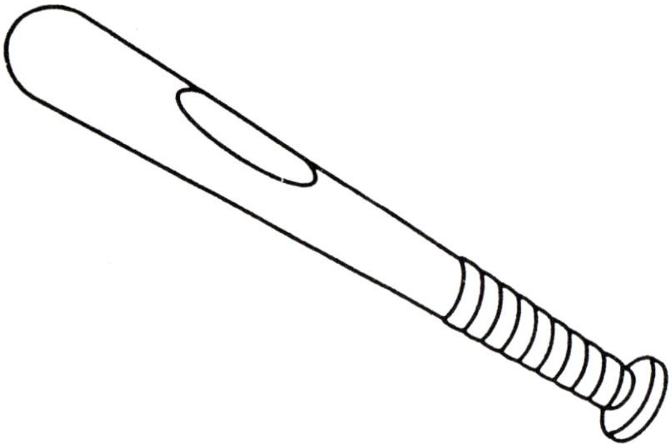

A

B

C

Draw a line from each picture to the letter that has the same beginning sound.

D

E

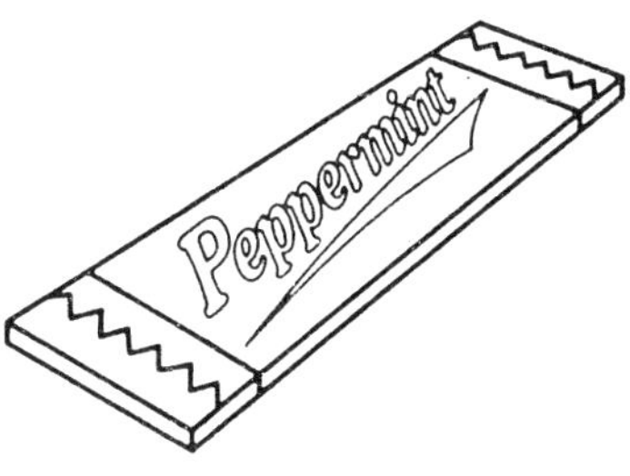

F

G

Draw a line from each picture to the letter that has the same beginning sound.

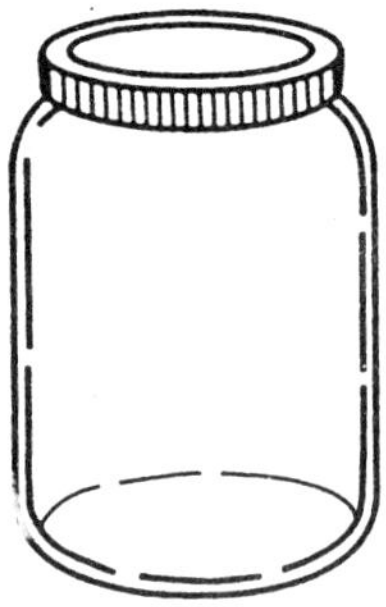

H

I

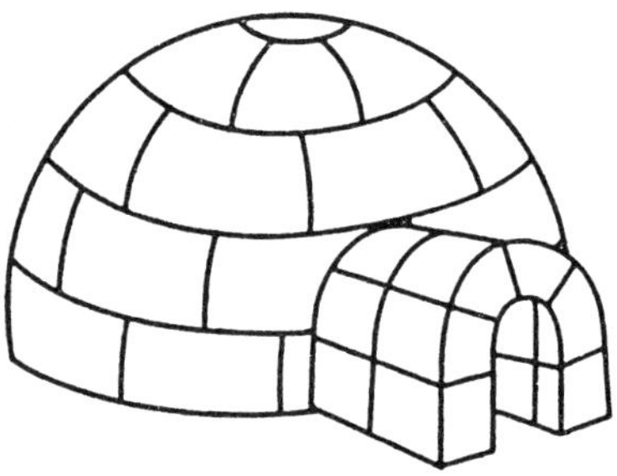

J

K

Draw a line from each picture to the letter that has the same beginning sound.

L

M

N

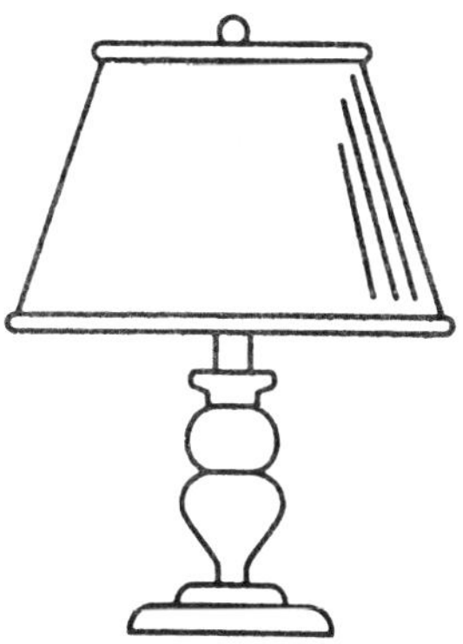

O

Draw a line from each picture to the letter that has the same beginning sound.

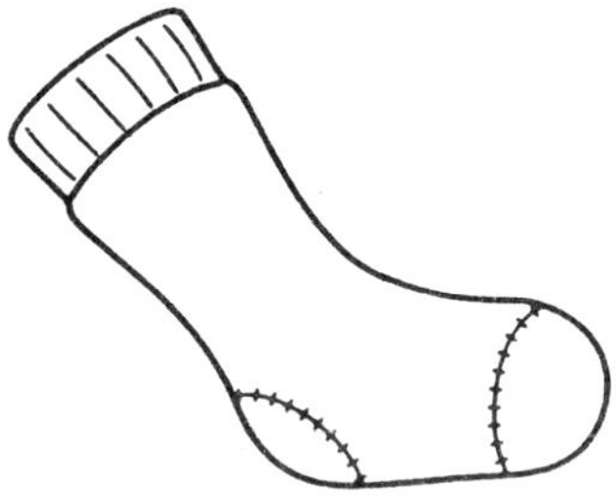

P

Q

R

S

Draw a line from each picture to the letter that has the same beginning sound.

T

U

V

W

Draw a line from each picture to the letter that has the same beginning sound.

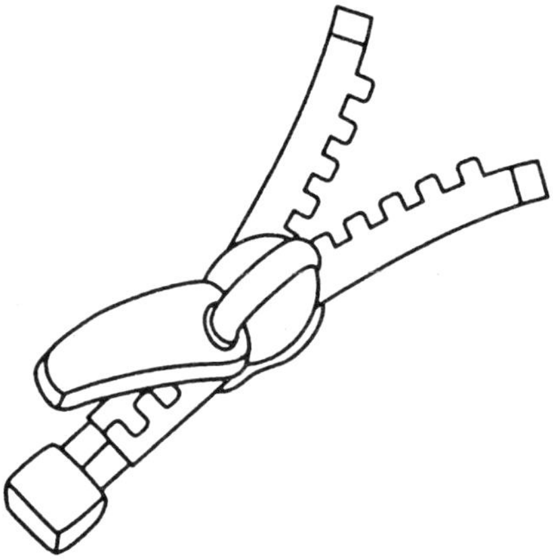

X

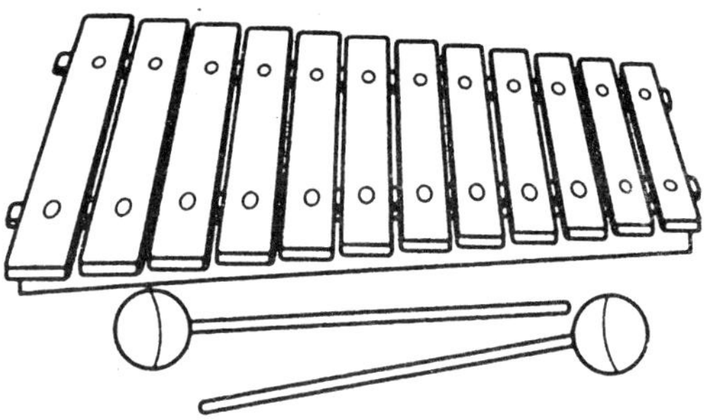

Y

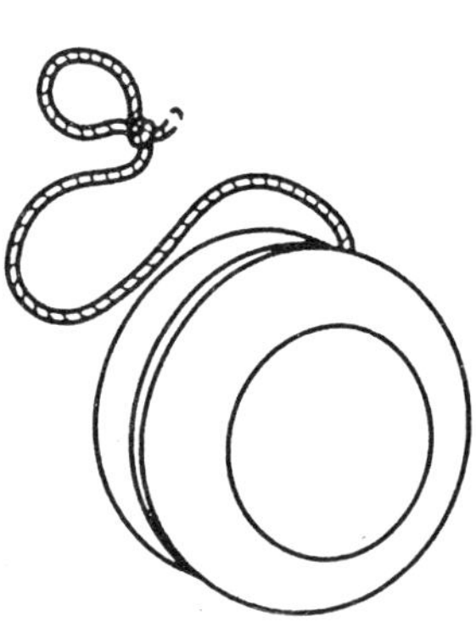

Z

Circle the letter that makes the beginning sound of each picture.

 h q	 k r
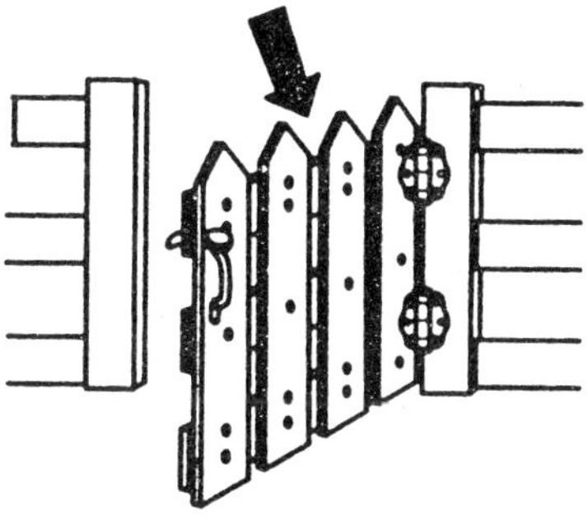 g z	 l y
 n s	 f v

Write the beginning letter of each word on the lines.

___at

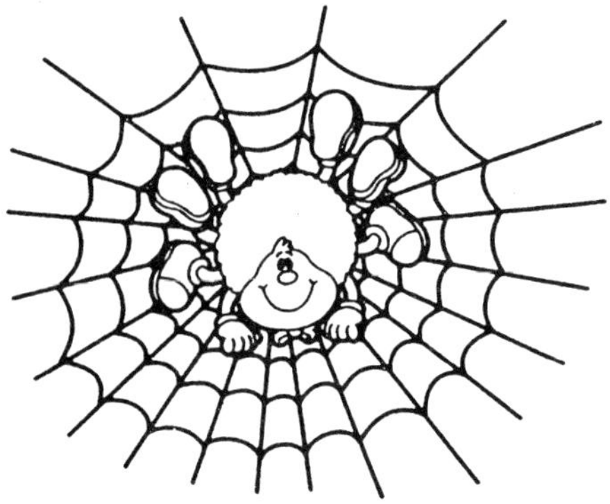

___eb

___ot

___ub

Write the beginning letter of each word on the lines.

ad

ig

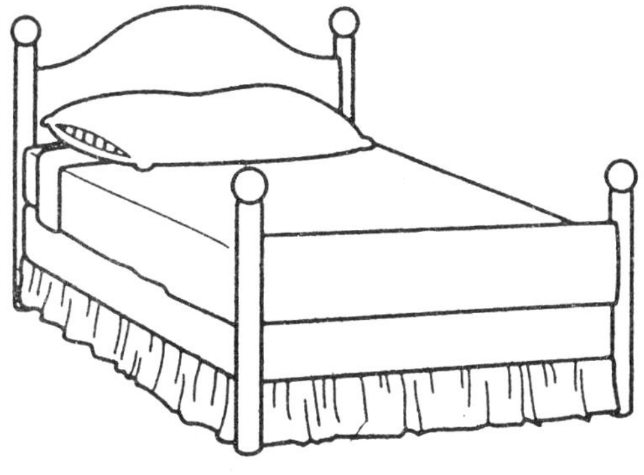

ed

og

Name the pictures below. Draw lines to connect the pictures whose names rhyme.

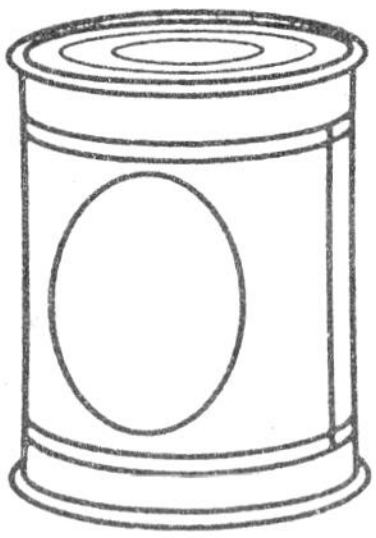

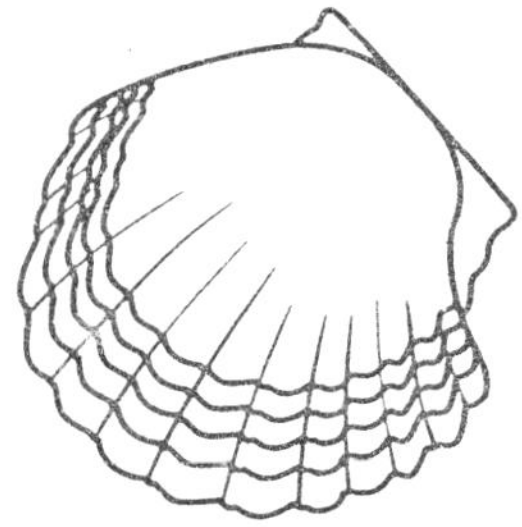

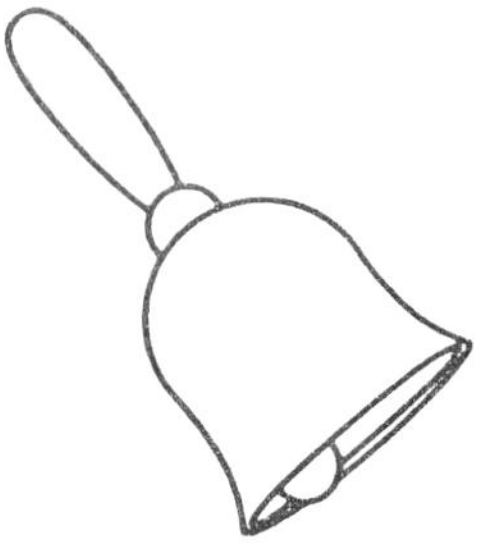

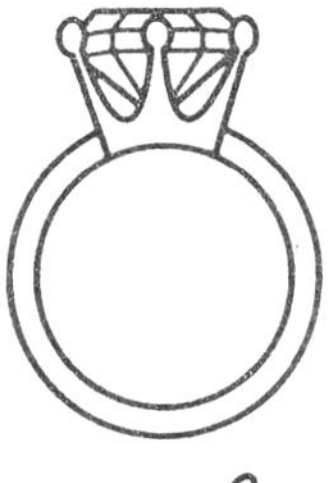

Name the pictures below. Draw lines to connect the pictures whose names rhyme.

q

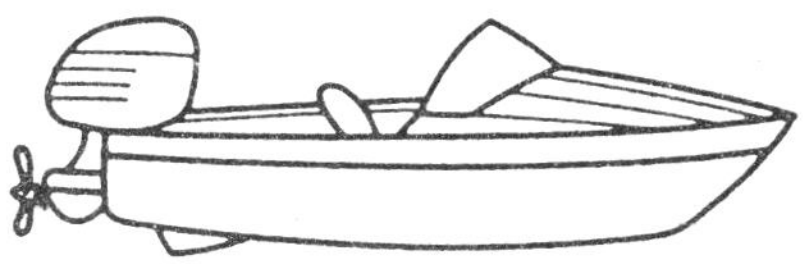

Look at the first picture in each row. Circle the picture that is the **same**.

Circle the two pictures in each row that are the **same**.

Look at the first picture in each row. Circle the picture that is **different**.

Kindergarten Activities Answer Key

Page 1
Lines should be traced from left to right.

Pages 2-4
Each capital letter should be traced and printed on the lines.

Page 5
Dots should be connected in order from A to Z to form a schoolhouse.

Pages 6-8
Each lowercase letter should be traced and printed on the lines.

Page 9
Dots should be connected in order from a to z to form an apple core.

Pages 10-12
The appropriate capital or lowercase letter should be printed for each letter of the alphabet

Page 13
Answers will vary.

Pages 14-15
Colour words should be traced and objects coloured the appropriate colours.

Pages 16-22
Lines should be drawn between each letter and the picture of the word that begins with that letter.

Page 23

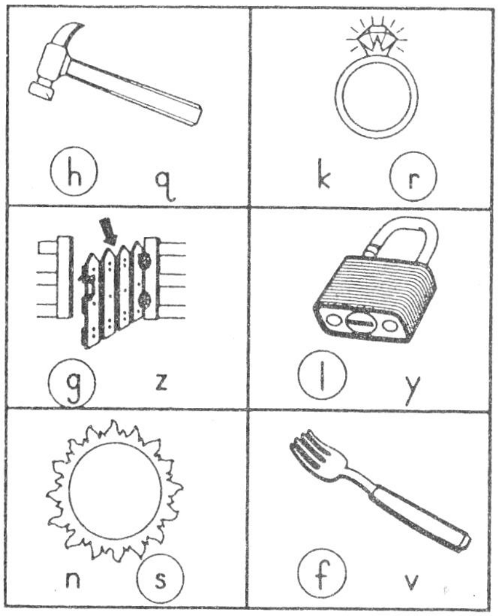

Pages 24-25
Beginning letters should be written to make the following words:

cat	web
pot	tub
sad	pig
bed	dog

Page 26

Page 27

Page 28

An X should be drawn on the matching picture in each row.

Page 29

The apes, gloves, first and last leaves, moons, and hammers should be circled.

Page 30

Page 31

Page 32

Page 33

An X should be drawn over the following items in each row: the second tree, the last building, the man.

Page 34

A line should be drawn between the following items: plane and clouds, car and road, train and tracks, boat and ocean.

Page 35

A line should be drawn between the following items: bird and nest, dog and doghouse, fish and bowl, cow and barn.

Page 36

A line should be drawn between the following items: umbrella/boots and cloud, t-shirt/shorts and sun, coat/mittens and snowflakes, pants/sweater and leaves.

Page 37

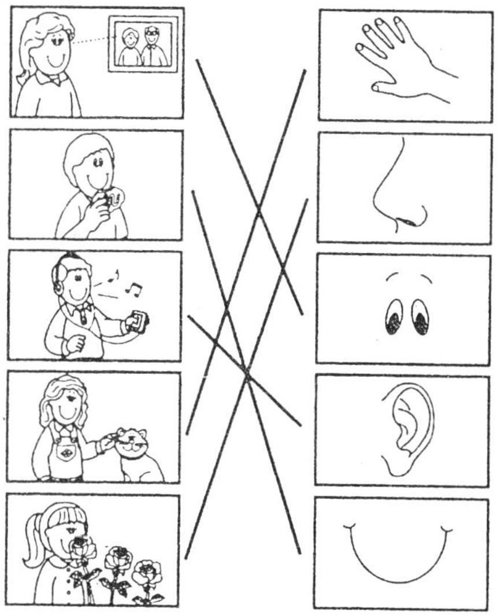

Page 38

The cheetah, rabbit, and fox should be coloured. The turtle, snail, and caterpillar should be circled.

Page 39

The candle, sun, and fire should be red. The ice, ice cream, and snowflake should be blue.

Page 40

The pillow, rabbit, and feather should be circled. An X should be drawn on the log, brick, and window.

Pages 41-42

Scenes in each row should be labeled as follows:

First row: 1, 3, 2
Second row: 3, 1, 2
Third row: 2, 1, 3
Page 42: (clockwise) 4, 1, 2, 3

Page 43

The shapes should be coloured according to the directions.

Page 44

The matching shape in each row should be coloured.

Page 45

Each number should be traced and printed on the lines.

Page 46

Dots should be connected in order from 0 to 10 to form a pencil.

Page 47

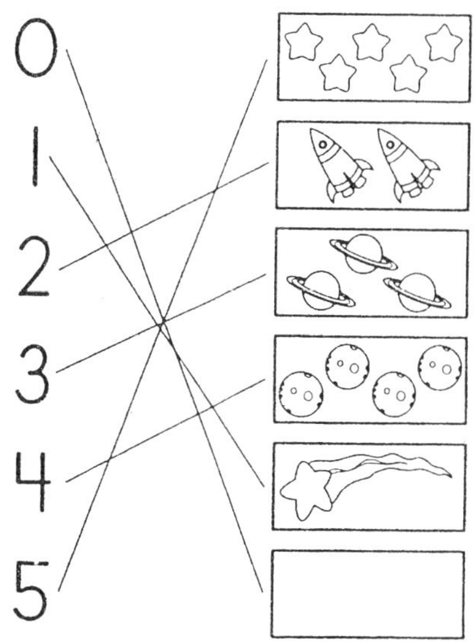

Page 48

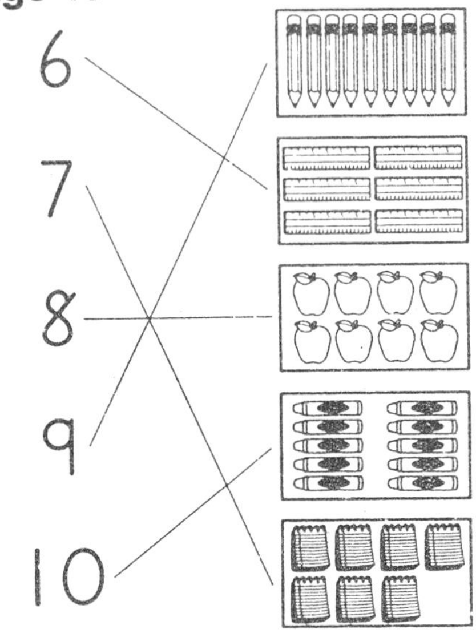

Pages 49-50

The correct number of objects should be coloured for the number in each row.

Pages 51-52

The correct number should be printed under each set of objects.

Pages 53-54

The appropriate set should be circled.

Page 55

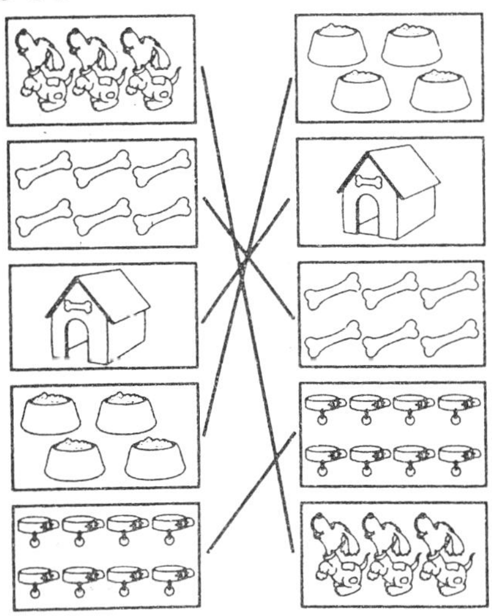

Page 56

Ducks should be coloured per directions.

Page 57

Times circled should be: 5:00, 8:00, 6:00, 12:00, 1:00, 11:00.

Page 58

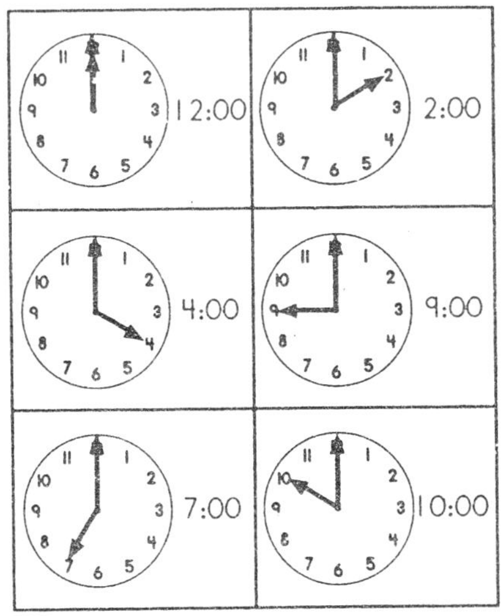

Page 59

Shoes equal 3 boxes, 4 boxes, 2 boxes.

Page 60

The following shapes complete the patterns:

First row: circle
Second row: oval
Third row: triangle
Fourth row: rectangle
Fifth row: triangle

Draw lines to connect the pictures of **opposites**.

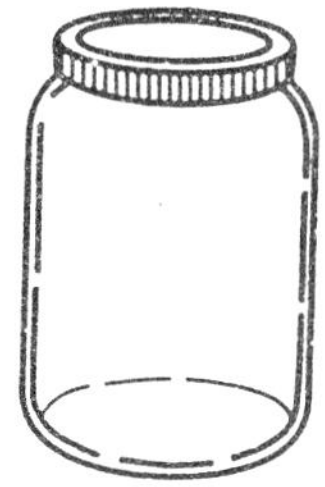

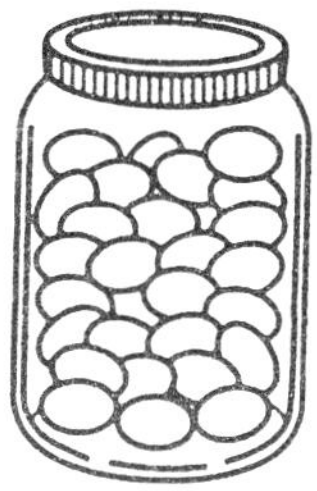

In each row, draw an X on the pictures that are big and circle the pictures that are small.

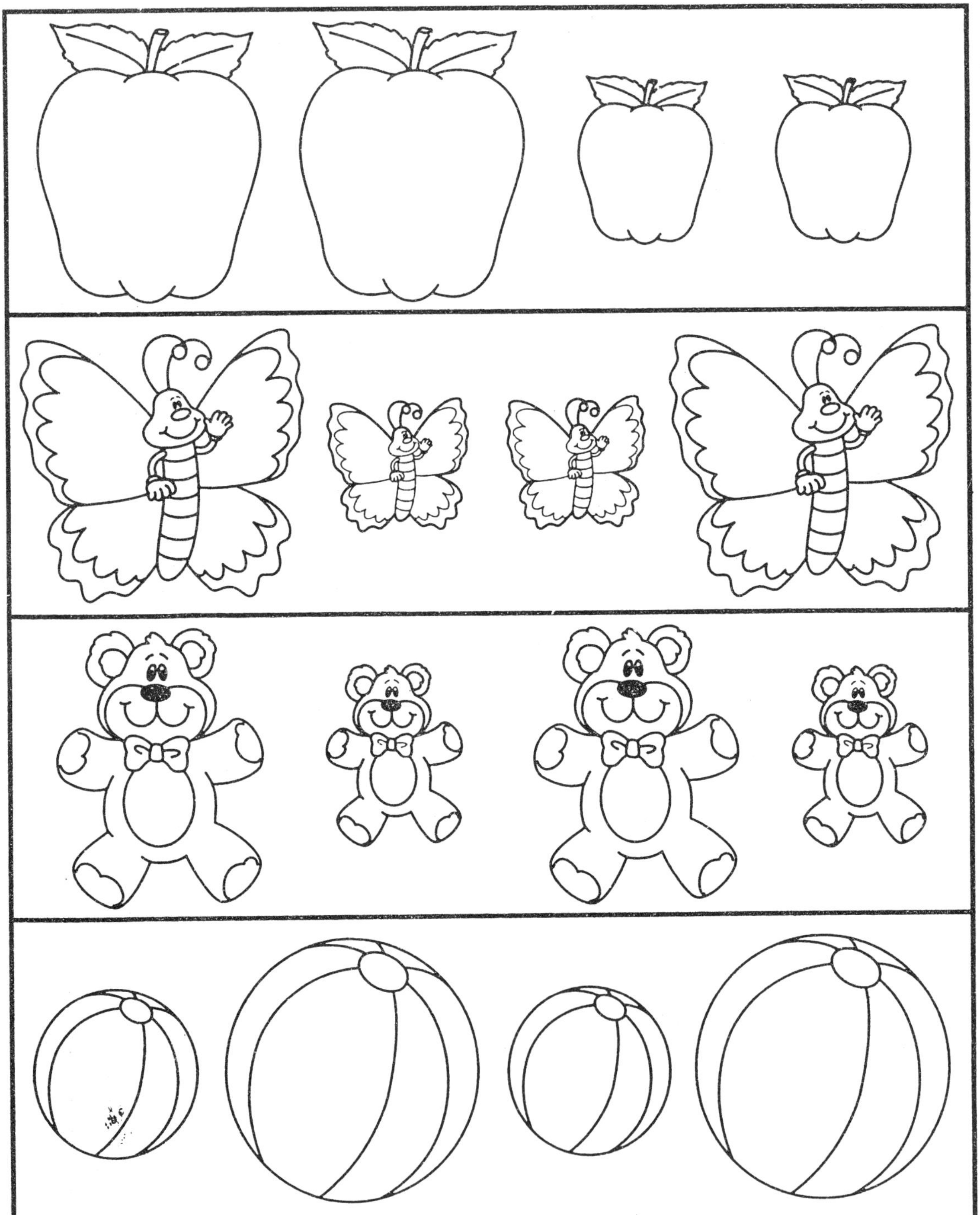

Look at the first picture in each row. Circle the picture that is taller than the first picture.

Draw a line to connect each form of transportation to the place where it travels.

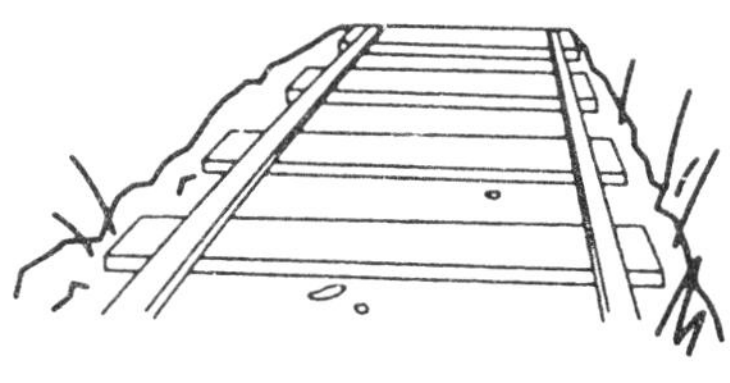

Draw a line to connect each animal to its home.

Draw a line to connect each set of clothing to the correct type of weather.

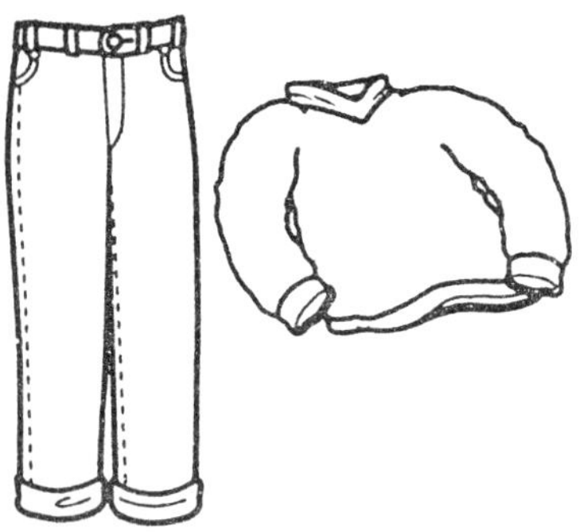

Draw a line to connect each sense to the correct body part.

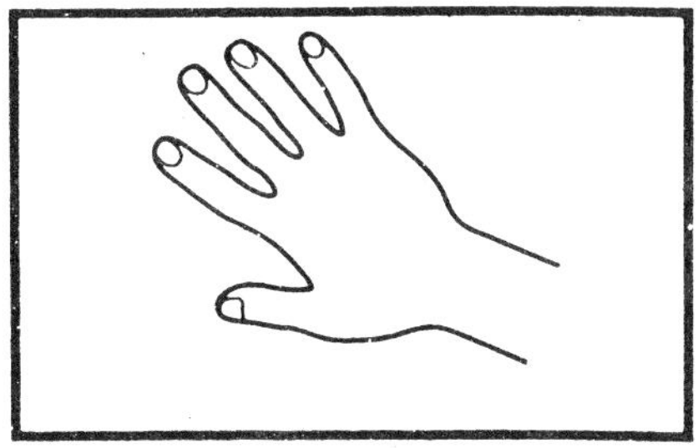

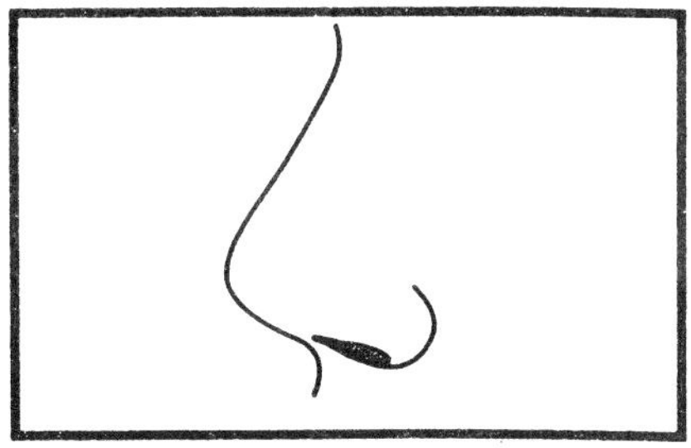

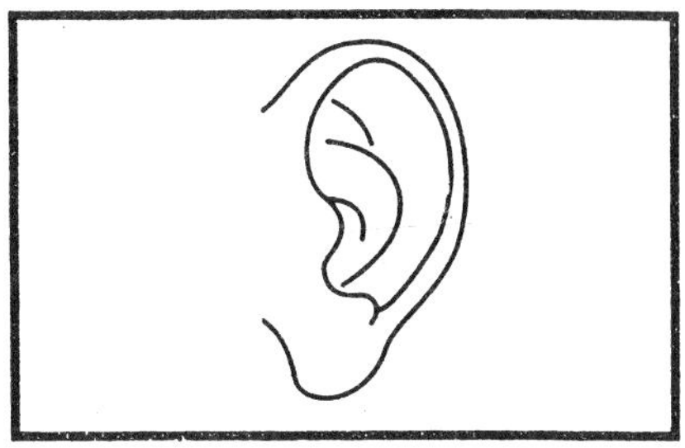

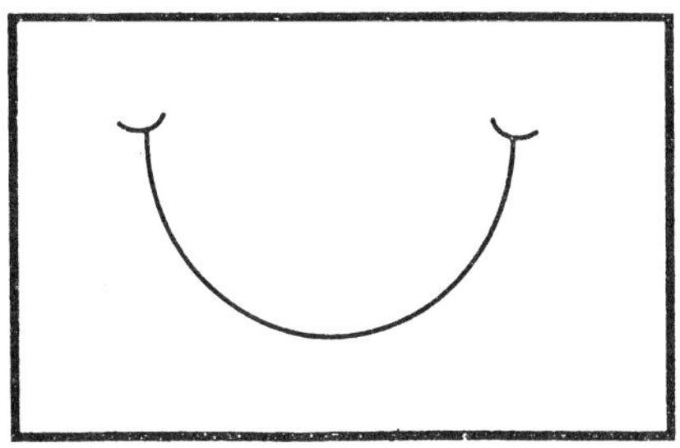

Colour the fast animals. Circle the slow animals.

Colour the hot objects red. Colour the cold objects blue.

Circle the soft objects. Draw an X on the hard objects.

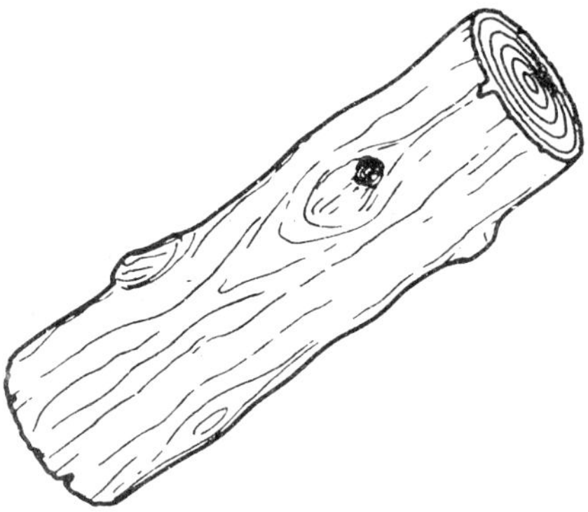

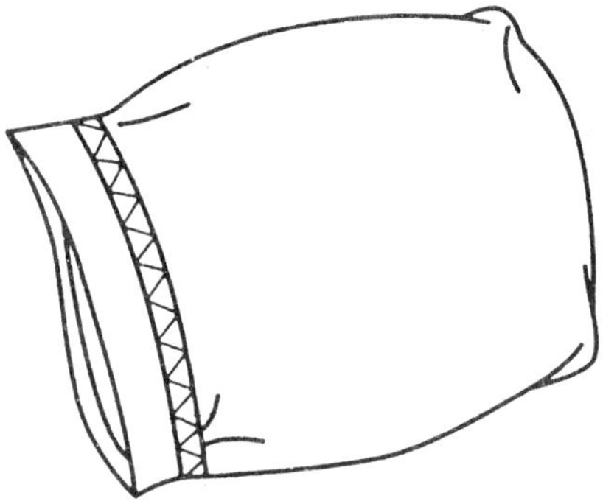

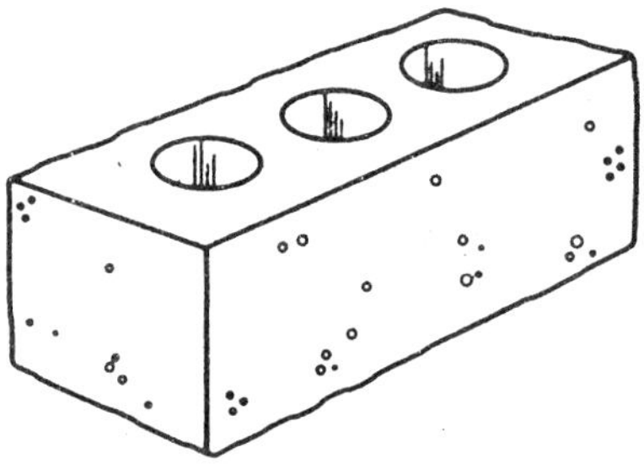

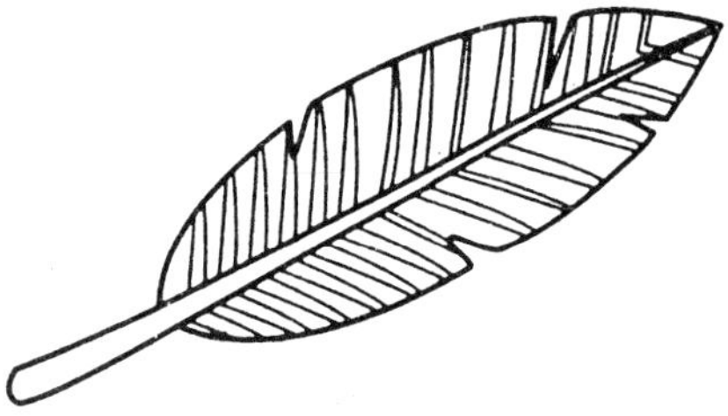

In each row, write 1, 2, or 3 in each box to put the scenes in the correct order.

Write 1, 2, 3, or 4 in each box to put the seasons in the correct order. The first season has been numbered for you.

Use the key to colour each shape.

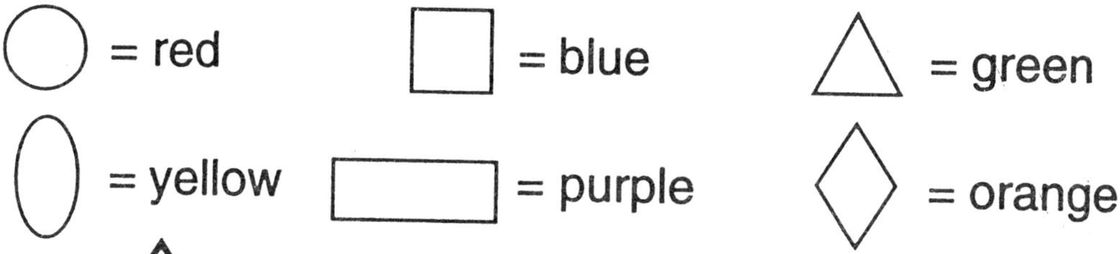

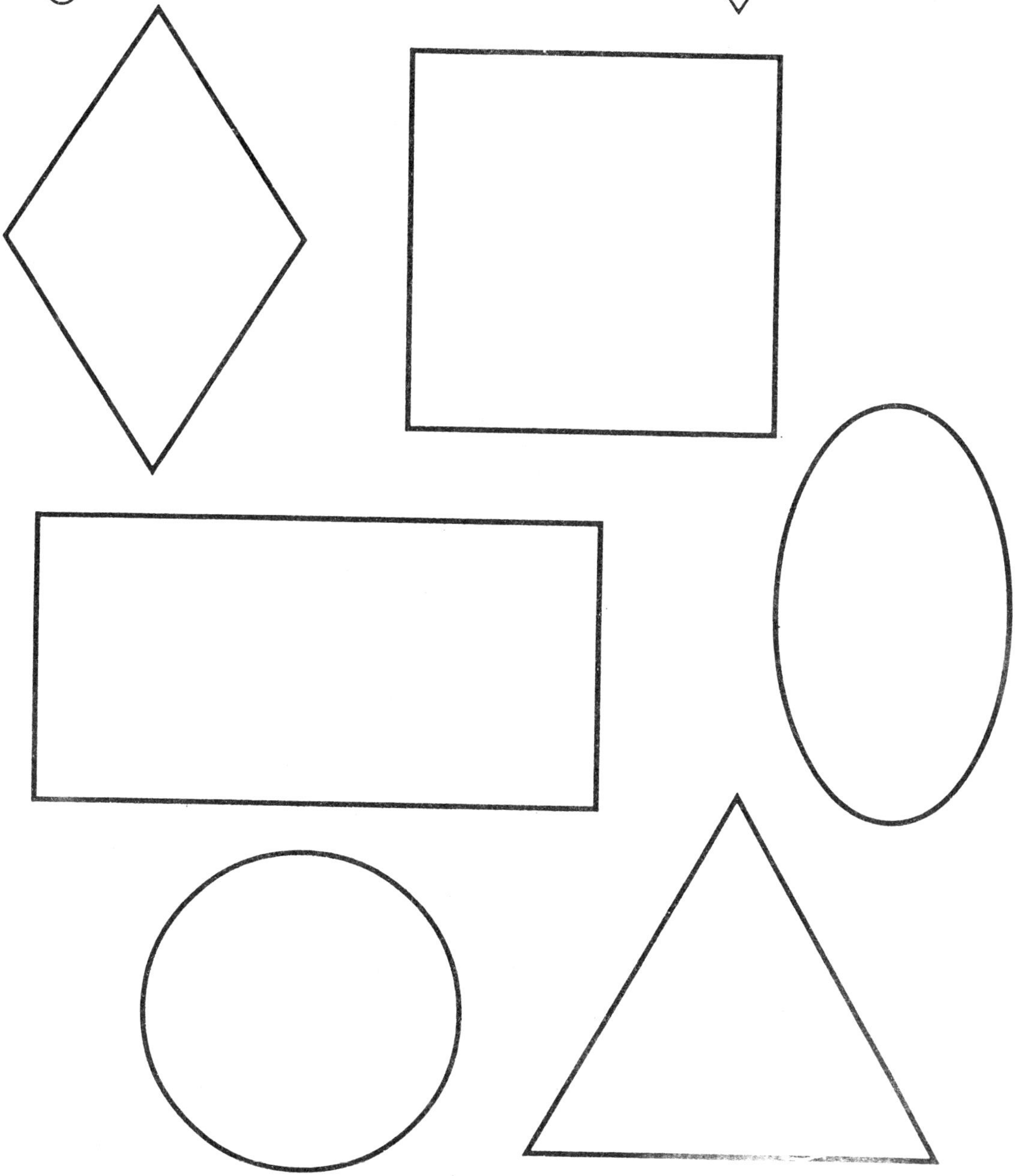

Look at the first shape in each row. Colour the shape in the row that is the same.

Trace and print each number.

0

1

2

3

4

5

6

7

8

9

Connect the dots. Begin at the ★. Continue in order from 0 to 10.

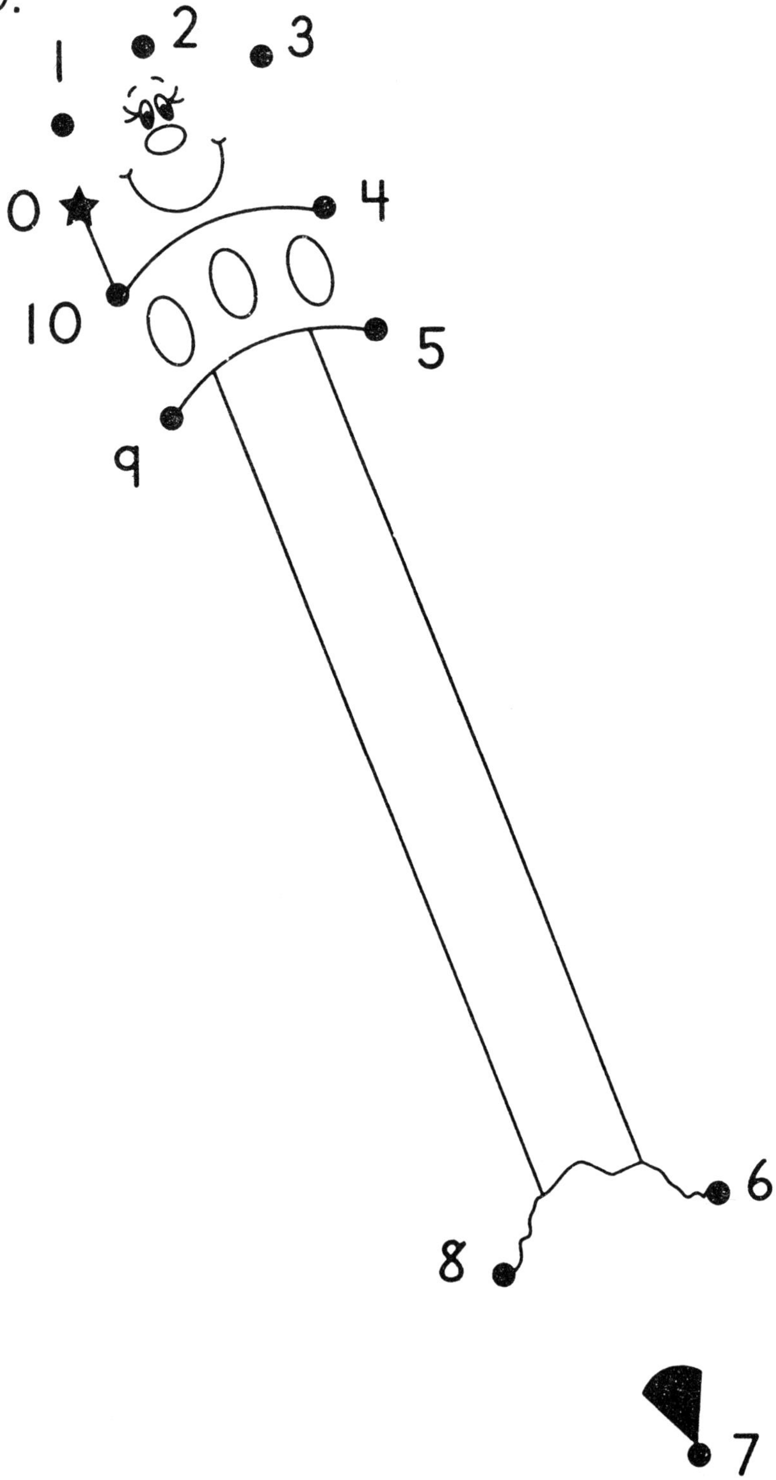

Draw a line to connect each number to the correct set.

0

1

2

3

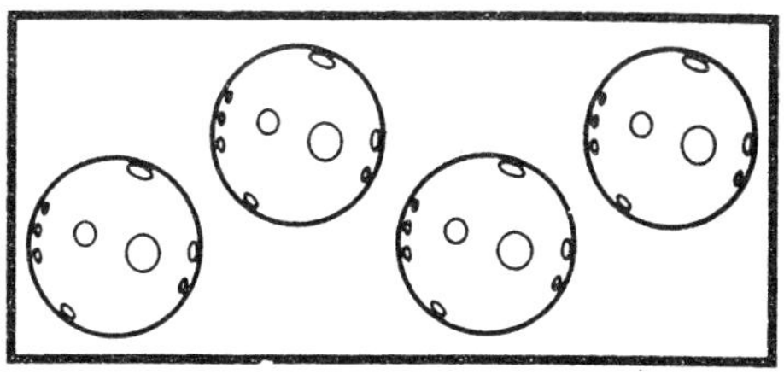

4

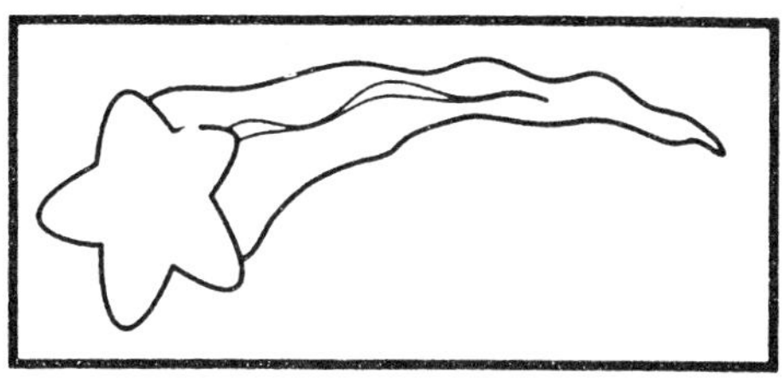

5

Draw a line to connect each number to the correct set.

6

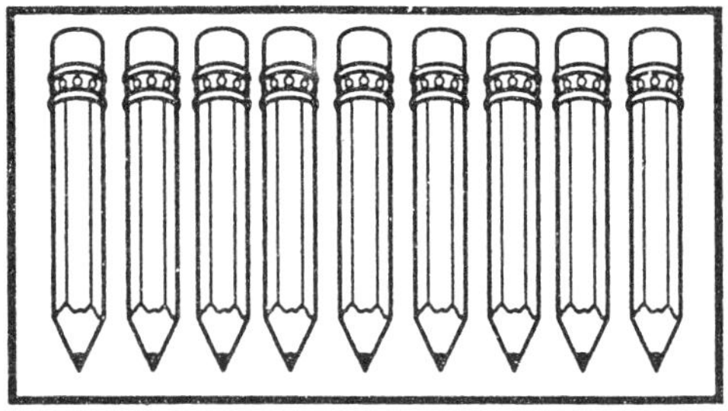

7

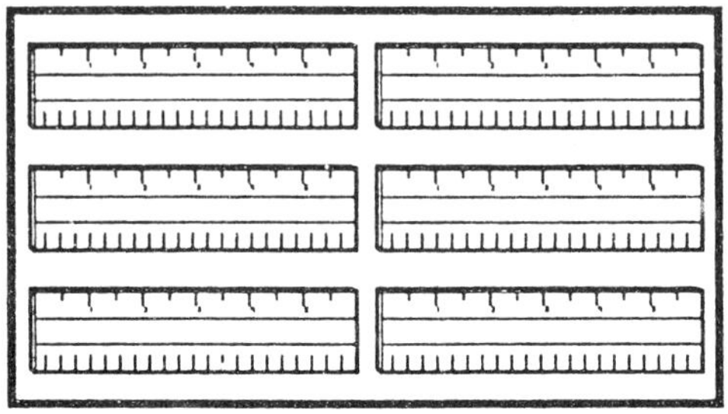

8

9

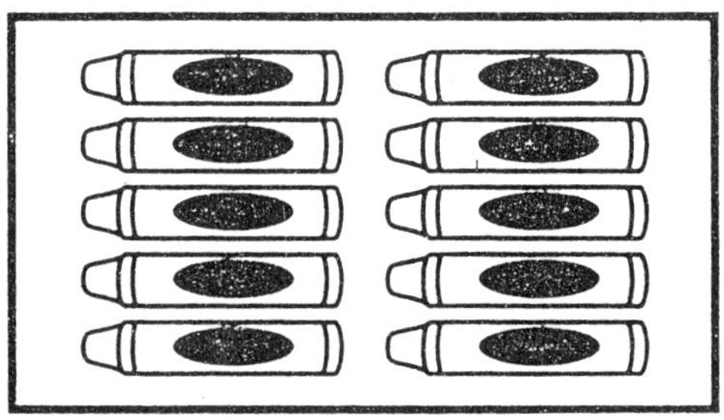

10

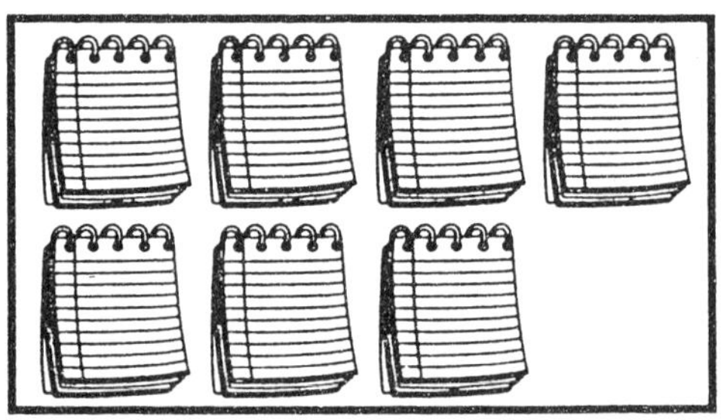

Read the number at the beginning of each row. Colour that many objects in the row.

3

5

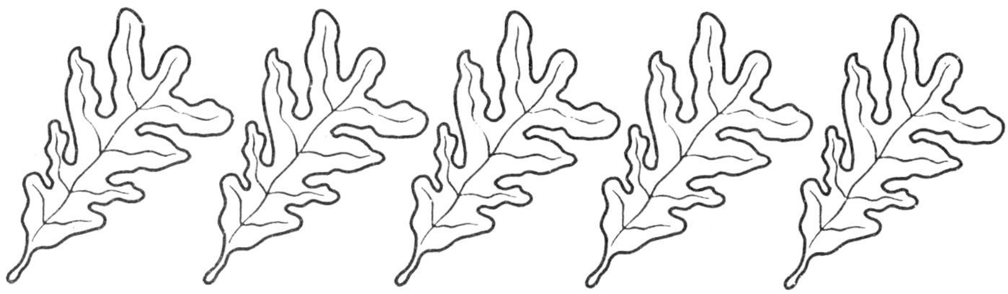

1

4

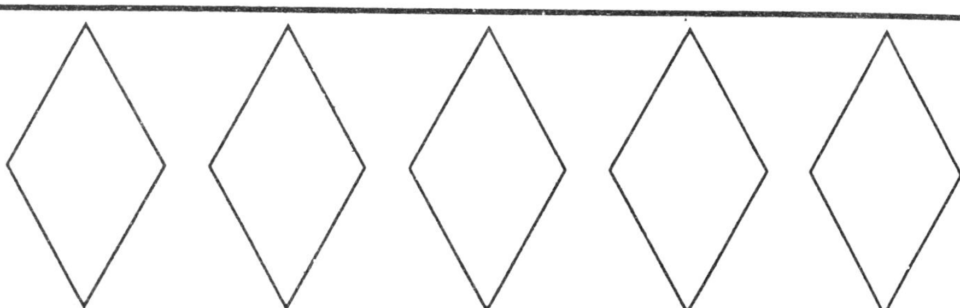

2

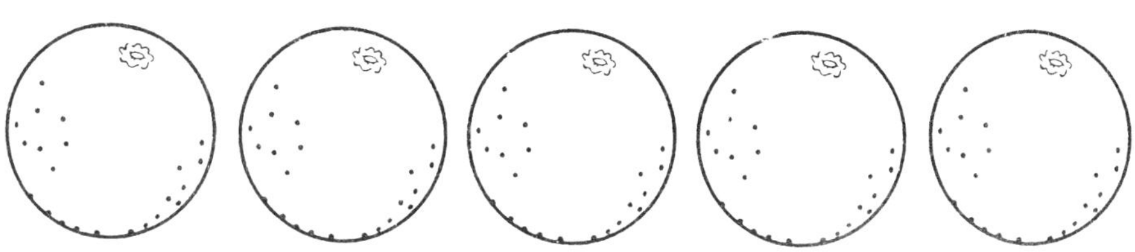

Read the number at the beginning of each row. Colour that many objects in the row.

8	
6	
9	
7	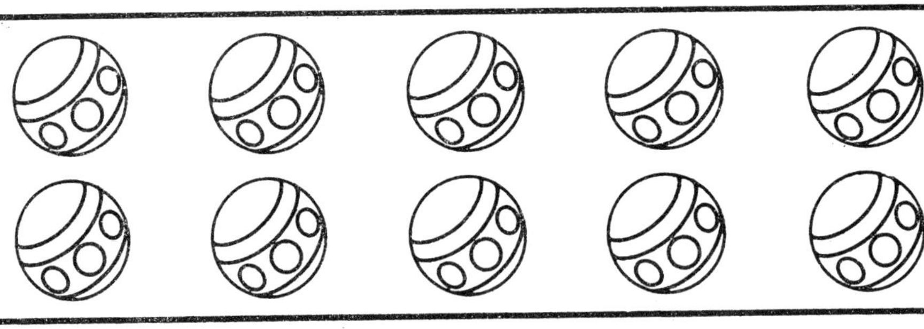
10	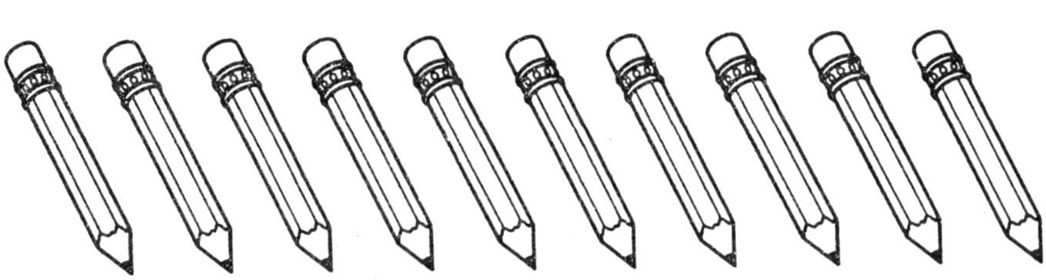

Count the number of objects in each box. Print the correct number on the lines.

Count the number of objects in each box. Print the correct number on the lines.

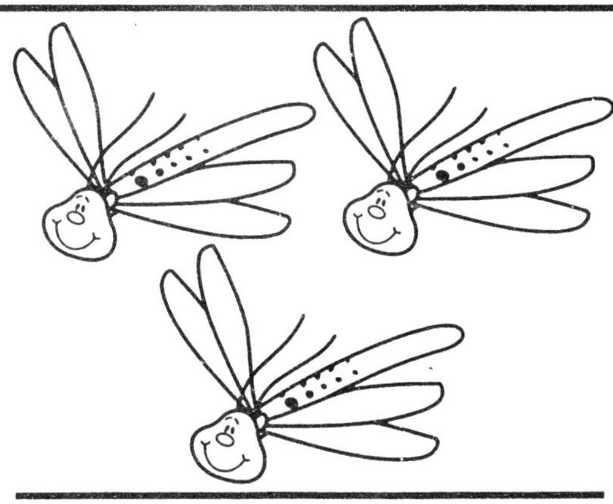

Count the sets in each box. Circle the set that has more objects.

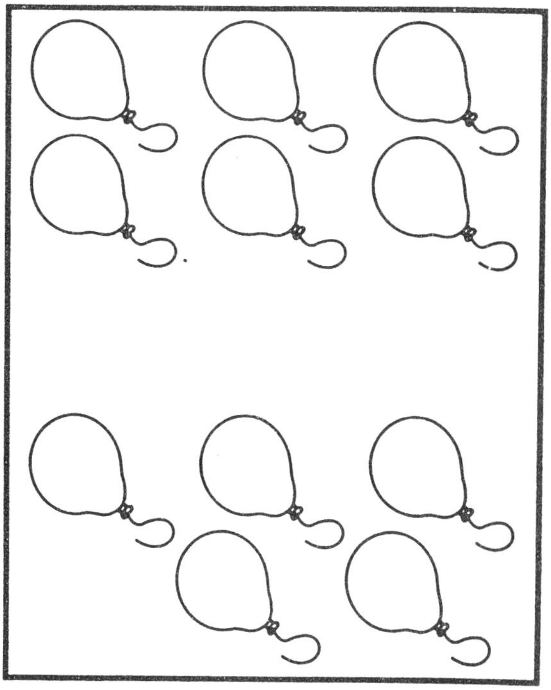

Count the sets in each box. Circle the set that has fewer objects.

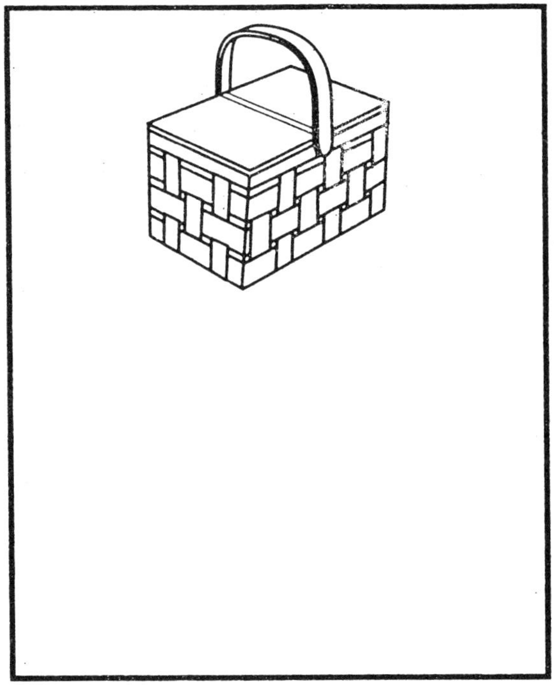

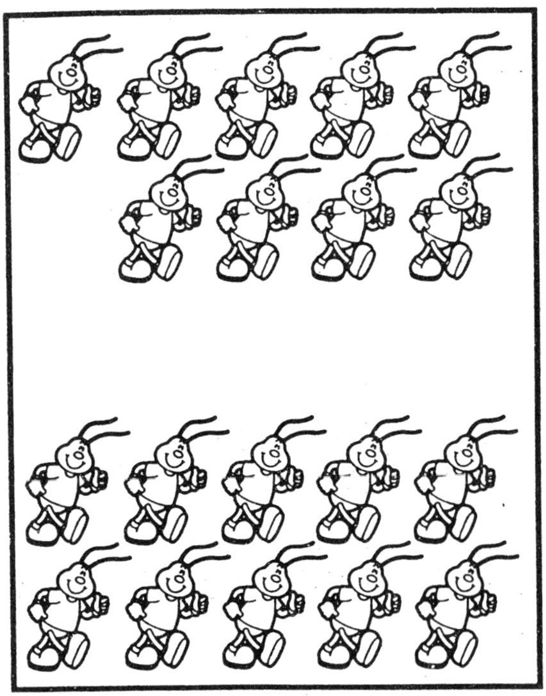

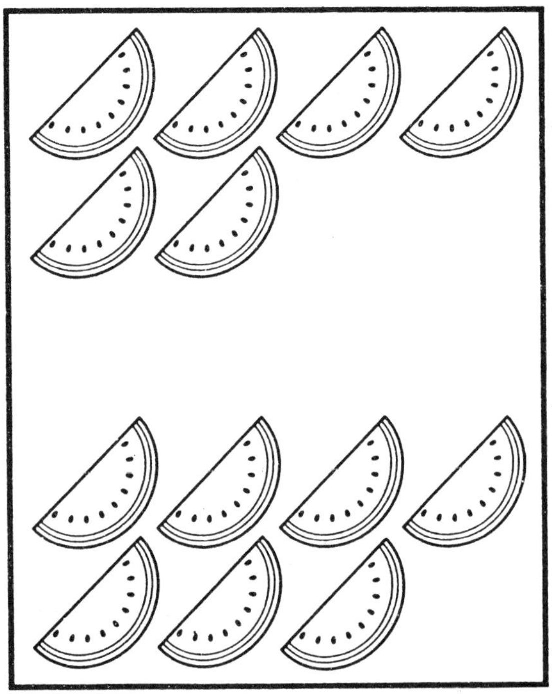

Draw lines to connect equal sets.

Colour the first duck red.

Colour the fifth duck orange.

Colour the fourth duck blue.

Colour the second duck green.

Colour the third duck yellow.

Circle the time that matches the time shown on each clock.

5:00

7:00

10:00

7:00

8:00

10:00

12:00

2:00

6:00

12:00

6:00

7:00

9:00

1:00

2:00

10:00

1:00

11:00

Draw hands on each clock to show the correct time.

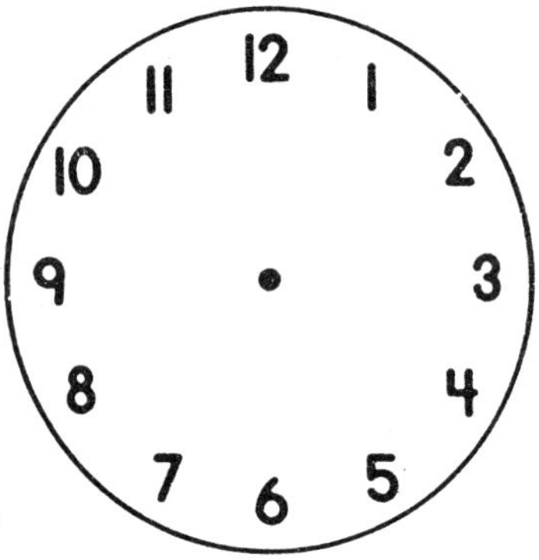

12:00

2:00

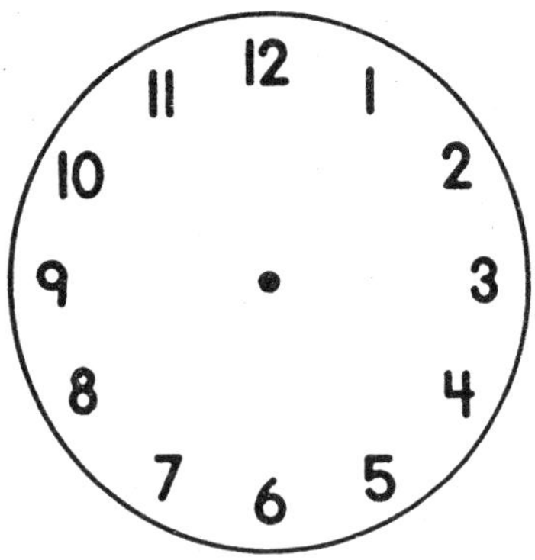

4:00

9:00

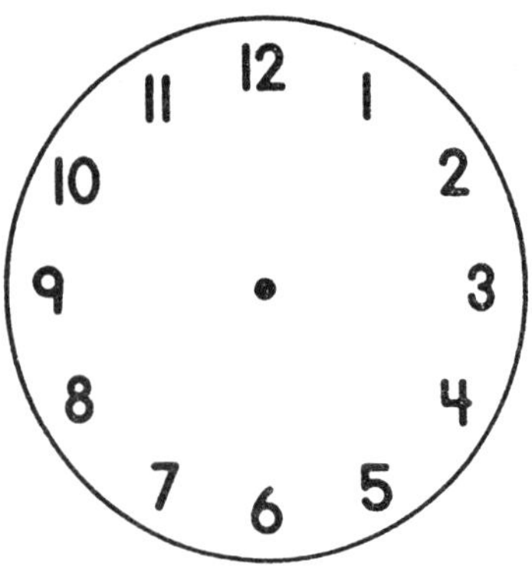

7:00

10:00

Measure the length of each shoe using the boxes below it.
Colour the boxes and write a number to show the length.

_________ boxes

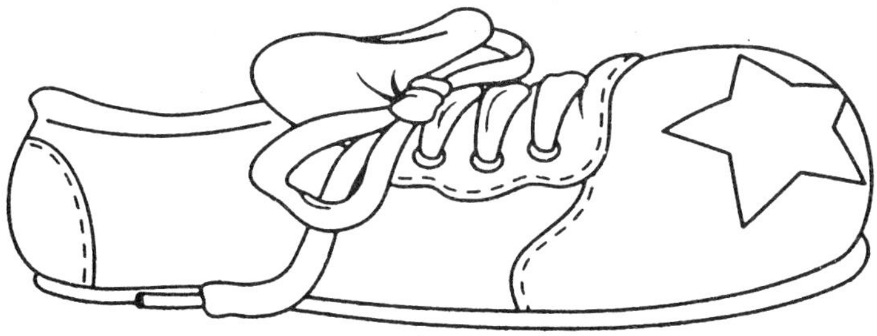

_________ boxes

_________ boxes

Draw the shape that comes next in each pattern.